# A History of the Floating Societies of the Christian Endeavor

First Fruits Press
*The Academic Open Press of Asbury Theological Seminary*
859-858-2236
first.fruits@asburyseminary.edu
http://place.asburyseminary.edu/firstfruits

Asbury Theological Seminary
204 N. Lexington Ave., Wilmore, KY 40390
asburyseminary.edu
800-2ASBURY

# A History of the
# Floating Societies
## of the
# Christian Endeavor

By

Robert A. Danielson

*First Fruits Press*
*Wilmore, Ky*
*c2014*

*A History of the Floating Societies of the Christian Endeavor*, by Robert A. Danielson

Published by First Fruits Press, © 2014

ISBN:9781621711421    (Print), 9781621711568 (Digital)

Digital version at http://place.asburyseminary.edu/academicbooks/8/

For all other uses, contact First Fruits Press:
859-858-2236
first.fruits@asburyseminary.edu

Danielson, Robert A. (Robert Alden), 1969-
     A history of the Floating Societies of the Christian Endeavor / by Robert A. Danielson.
     viii, 67 p. :ill., ports, ; 21 cm.
     Wilmore, Ky. : First Fruits Press, c2014.
     ISBN: 9781321711421 (pbk.)
     1. Floating Society of Christian Endeavor -- History. 2. Sailors -- Religious life. 3. Seafaring life -- Religious aspects -- Christianity. I. Title.
   BV1428.F6 D36 2014

Cover design by Wes Wilcox

# Table of Contents

# Images

# Dedication

This work is dedicated to those courageous enough to develop creative methods in pursuit of the kingdom of God. Men like Madison Edwards and women like Antoinette Jones are a constant inspiration. It is from small ideas that great results flourish.

This book is also dedicated to the unknown sailors of the Floating Christian Endeavor who helped build the kingdom of God in ways that we may never know.

# Dedication

# Acknowledgments

I would like to express my deep thanks and appreciation for those who helped in this endeavor, even if they are not aware of the role they played. Special thanks go to my grandparents, Miriam and George Wiseman, who kept this story alive, preserved the photographs for posterity, and passed that heritage down to me. Along with this, I want to thank Grace Yoder and the B.L. Fisher Library Archives and Special Collections at Asbury Theological Seminary, for helping me preserve this collection for future generations and use it for this book. I also want to thank Dr. Art McPhee of Asbury Theological Seminary for reading the paper this book is based on and giving me valuable feedback.

In addition, I humbly express thanks to all of the women mentors in my life, but especially Dr. Eunice Irwin, whose focus on women in mission always helped me be aware of the key role women like Antoinette Jones played in mission history. She taught me not to pass over their valuable contributions.

Last, but certainly not least, I would like to express my great love and eternal devotion to my wife, Kelly Godoy de Danielson, without whom any of my work would be impossible. Her encouragement, love, and keen intellectual insight constantly help me become a better person and missiologist every day.

*Chapter 1*

# Early Religion Work for Seafarers

*Some went out on the sea in ships;*
*they were merchants on the mighty*
*waters. They saw the works of*
*the Lord, his wonderful deeds in*
*the deep.(Psalm 107:23-24)*

The life of the sailor has never been easy. Throughout much of history, men who went to sea were facing immense dangers, sickness, and isolation from the places they called home. Life in port cities was full of danger as well. Prostitution, gambling, and alcohol all provided ways for sailors to spend their pay before another dangerous journey. Spiritual guidance was usually limited to work on the shore. Some Catholic churches were devoted to saints who protected maritime communities and isolated ministers in port churches would preach sermons for the women and families left behind. In a few rare occasions, ministry went on to the ships with priests or religious captains who read lessons and prayers on the Sabbath. But a concerted, systematic attempt to minister to the needs of this marginalized group was often missing. Sailors were seen as unregenerate and non-religious, simply living for the next hedonistic moment they were free in port.

It was out of religious reform movements in the 18th century that things began to change. Kverndal notes,

> Both the Methodist Revival in Britain and the Colonial counterpart in America had, in essence, been mission-oriented from the start. Now, as specific societies for world mission multiplied on both sides of the Atlantic, it was inevitable that zealous missionaries should "discover" the men on whom they must rely for both transportation and communication. No sooner had bridgeheads been established overseas, however, than missionary societies sensed an even more urgent stimulus. Seamen coming from supposedly "Christian" countries could, with one drunken spree ashore, effectively nullify any positive impact that months of patient missionary endeavor might have made on the local native population. Here, surely, was a missionary challenge of the highest priority: the evangelization of the seafarer.[1]

The first half of the 19th century was an unparalleled age of ships and the movement of people and goods across the oceans, yet the life of the sailor had not improved much. Because of their

---

1    Roald Kverndal, *Seamen's Missions: Their Origin and Early Growth* (Pasedena, CA: William Carey Library, 1986):45.

transitory work, they were unable to integrate well into local communities. Working as a sailor was a task for lower classes that were often trapped by poverty. In port towns, young men might be forced into service on ships to face unhealthy living conditions and poor quality food. Fresh water supplies became stale so quickly that they were mixed with alcohol, usually rum, to make it more palatable, and this ration of "grog" was vital to survival, even if it led to frequent fighting and alcoholism. On top of this, brutal flogging was practiced onboard ships as a frequent method of punishment.

Additional problems had to deal with pay. Without bank accounts or safe ways of keeping money, it was simply easier to spend the money earned on a long voyage in port than to try and save it for an unknown future. Along with this came the difficulties of communication as sailors had no stable address or the ability to forward mail, assuming they had learned to even read or write at all. Newspapers and popular reading material was rarely available and so the sailors remained cutoff from the larger culture and current events.

The Naval and Military Bible Society began in 1779 as a way to distribute scriptures to men in the British navy, and was followed by the British and Foreign Bible Society in 1804. The distribution of other religious literature fell to the Society for Promoting Christian Knowledge (an Anglican organization founded in 1698) and then the Religious Tract Society in 1799. With the presence of religious materials and Bibles, local preachers with local societies began to form in the early

1800's focusing on the spiritual needs of seafarers in the port cities. The first unified effort was the British and Foreign Seamen's Friend Society and Bethel Union founded in 1819. With the growth of the Bethel Movement, a special flag was used to call meetings on board ships in port, with the approval of sympathetic captains. Experimental floating churches were tried in a few ports and meanwhile the published material available for sailors grew at a tremendous rate.

In the early 1800's an expanding religious concern for mariners began to grow along the Northeast coast of the United States.[2] In the United States, the first focused effort was the Boston Society for the Religious and Moral Improvement of Seamen, founded in 1812. However with the War of 1812 and other complications it ended in 1817. While work in various ports continued, with a strong influence from Britain and the Bethel Movement, the American Seamen's Friend Society was not founded until 1826 in New York. Similarly in Britain, larger nondenominational agencies began to form, such as the Seamen's Christian Friend Society in 1846.

Local missions in both British and American organizations began to establish libraries and reading rooms for sailors in port, and look for other ways to provide additional positive forms of recreation. Social awareness also increased

---

2    For more information see Roald Kverndal, *Seamen's Missions: Their Origin and Early Growth* (Pasedena, CA: William Carey Library, 1986). Also, *The Way of the Sea: The Changing Shape of Mission in the Seafaring World* (Pasedena, CA: William Carey Library, 2008).

in terms of education, care of sailor's orphans and widows, and the need to help and assist unemployed, abandoned, or shipwrecked sailors. Temporary housing, hospitals, and asylums began to be formed to meet some of these needs. But for all of this work, the focus was still on work on land in various ports to meet sailors' spiritual needs, not on any type of work at sea.

The history of religious work on government ships in the United States is fairly well known.[3] Navy chaplains were first commissioned in the Continental Navy in 1778 to serve the needs of men at sea by reading prayers and conducting funerals. However, these early chaplains were few in number, and until World War I, they were limited to only 24 chaplains.   Chaplains were frequently poorly trained and more focused on educating young midshipmen then providing spiritual support   to the crew. During World War I the Chaplain Corps of the United States Navy grew to more than 200 chaplains, but the largest increase came in World War II, when there were as many as 2,981 chaplains serving with the U.S. Navy. Before this period, any other ministry to sailors was left to the mission outreach of the local churches in port.

In the United States, the work (centered in New York and Boston) by the American Seaman's Friend Society and the Bethel Movement had established land-based ministries to serve the spiritual needs of sailors. All of this spiritual work also led to seeking

---

3    Clifford Merrill Drury, *The History of the Chaplain Corps, United States Navy, Vol. 3. United States Navy Chaplains* (Washington DC: U.S. Government Printing Office, 1948), i.

social reforms in the U.S. Navy, such as ending the practices of grog rationing and flogging. These actions laid the groundwork for a revival movement among sailors on board Navy ships, known as the American Naval Awakening (1858-1865). This would be the first organized, lay-led, spiritual movement conducted on board ships at sea, as well as in port.

Beginning with a converted sailor, John Morris, who asked to lead a prayer meeting on the U.S. Receiving Ship *North Carolina* on November 21, 1858, revival came to the sailors of the U.S. Navy. One of the key problems was the temporary nature of ship assignments, although this was also an unexpected missionary asset. Kverndal notes, "But this fragmentation of fellowship proved only a precondition of mobility and growth. Within six months, 'little bands of sailor missionaries' had been planted in a score of widely scattered United States ships."[4] Rev. Charles J. Jones of the New York Mariners' Church worked to maintain some type of correspondence and cohesion for this early movement, but the movement itself seems to have ended with the closing of the American Civil War. While there are no clear connections between the American Naval Awakening and the Floating Christian Endeavor, many of the ideas from the Awakening would be built upon by the future Floating Christian Endeavor to carry ministry out onto the ships themselves.

---

4    Kverndal, *Seamen's Missions: Their Origin and Early Growth,* 531.

*Chapter 2*

# The Founding
# of the Floating
# Christian Endeavor

*Sing to the Lord a new song, his
praise from the ends of the earth,
you who go down to the sea, and
all that is in it, you islands, and all
who live in them. (Isaiah 42:10)*

On February 2, 1881, Dr. Francis Clark, a
Congregational minister in Portland, Maine,
gathered a group of young people together in the
parsonage parlor to begin a new society. This was a
society of youth, a radical new idea in the church at
that time. One article describes Dr. Clark's thought
this way,

> From long and earnest thought he had
> decided that what the church needed was
> not more pink teas and oyster suppers,
> with which to allure young people, but
> a higher ideal for organized work, a
> nobler conception of what Christian
> manhood and womanhood should mean,

> a translation into twentieth century life
> and activity of that impulse by means
> of which Peter the Hermit long ago
> organized the Crusades- and so changed
> the geography of Europe.[5]

The society organized into various committees around a constitution intending to make the youth more committed and devoted to serving God. Members were required to sign a pledge that required them to participate in every meeting. This small, organized group in the parsonage parlor began to grow as youth took a greater interest in the work of the church. By 1906, there were almost three million members in 66,000 societies all over the world, from Africa, China, India, and Brazil to the United States, Canada, and England.

One evening in 1890, at the meeting of a local Christian Endeavor Society at the First Congregational Church in Falmouth, Massachusetts, Antoinette Palmer Jones, the secretary of the local society, met with Madison Edwards, a local man who went on board ships to preach and minister to sailors. They discussed adapting the Christian Endeavor Society pledge and program to meet the unique needs of sailors. Antoinette Jones sent the idea to the Christian Endeavor headquarters in Boston and was given permission from the society to try out this new idea.

5    From Mary Caroline Crawford, "The World for Christ." *National Magazine*, February 1906: 474.

*Dr. Francis E. Clark, Founder
of Christian Endeavor*[6]
Image in the Public Domain.

Neither of these co-founders could have achieved this on their own. Madison Edwards was the son of a sea captain of a lighthouse relief supply ship. He knew the sea and the men who worked on the sea. When he was sixteen he began asking permission to go aboard ships and preach to

---

6   From Crawford, "The World for Christ," pp. 473.

the sailors.[7] He knew their needs, their concerns, and he shared their life. He was not the greatest scholar, but was rather a devout man of action. Antoinette Palmer Jones was a single seamstress who would never marry. She lived with her parents and took care of their needs. She knew little about sailors and their lives, but she was a woman of committed faith and great intelligence. Her father, a professor of chemistry, had his eyes damaged by a lab explosion, and Antoinette even patented an invention of a writing tablet for people with limited or no vision.[8]

Madison Edwards and Antoinette Palmer Jones both attended the First Congregational Church in Falmouth, and both were involved in the Christian Endeavor Society. Edwards requested help in his ministry to sailors and the Christian Endeavor Society of the church worked to help him. As it happened, Jones lived closest to the telegraph office, and became the first person to be contacted by Edwards from Woods Hole if he needed assistance. According to Showalter,

> One night a ship came in. Edwards called for help, and Antoinette was the only Christian Endeavor member able to go. So Antoinette bravely went all by herself. It was so dark that night that she had to trust her horse to find its own

7 George Wiseman, *They Kept the Lower Lights Burning: The Story of the Seaman's Bethel and its Chaplains* (Orlando, FL: Daniels Publishers, 1976), 18-19. http://place.asburyseminary.edu/academicbooks/1/

8 Douglas K. Showalter, "Antoinette Palmer Jones: The Goodness and Power of One Christian," *Spiritsail* 25(2) 2011, page 24.

way to Woods Hole. Antoinette was very
willing to give herself to help others. At
this time she was beginning to realize
how much she really loved this type of
ministry to sailors.[9]

The first Floating Christian Endeavor Society
was established sometime in 1890. Wiseman[10]
indicates that the first society was established on
the Revenue Cutter *Gallatin,* although Showalter[11]
points to church records, where Antoinette Jones
recorded the establishment of a society on May
12, 1890 on the Revenue Cutter *Dexter.* The record
notes, "On May 12th, members of the Society went
to Wood's Holl[12] to meet the crew of the Cutter
'Dexter' and assist in the formation of a 'floating'
Society of Christian Endeavor. Such a society was
perfected May 12th. Antoinette P. Jones, Sec."
About a month later Antoinette Jones was named
Superintendant of the Floating Christian Endeavor.

9    Showalter, "Antoinette Palmer Jones: The Goodness and
     Power of One Christian," 26.
10   Wiseman, *They Kept the Lower Lights Burning: The Story
     of the Seaman's Bethel and its Chaplains:* 35.
11   Showalter, "Antoinette Palmer Jones: The Goodness and
     Power of One Christian," 26.
12   This is an early variant of the place today known as Woods
     Hole.

*Early Image of Madison Edwards*
From the Author's Collection

*Pen Sketch of Miss Antoinette Jones*[13]
Image in the Public Domain.

While Jones was the organizing influence, the idea and practical side of the work was Edwards'. In the early years, the local Christian Endeavor Society of the Falmouth Congregational Church worked to help Madison Edwards with his work on the local vessels. They continued to use his boat, the *Helen May* to go out and visit larger vessels in the harbor in the early work of the Floating Societies as well.

13  Anonymous, "A Pioneer in 'Floating' Work", *San Francisco Call*, 82:43 (13 July, 1897), 3.

*The Helen May in its Days in Woods Hole*
Courtesy of B.L. Fisher Library Archives, Asbury Theological Seminary.

Mary Jenkins was the daughter of a sea captain and she grew up on board ship. Over time, she became a schoolteacher at Woods Hole and was involved with the Christian Endeavor Society in the Falmouth Congregational Church. In a speech recorded in the *Sea Breeze*, she relates the story of her early involvement as an assistant to Madison Edwards,

> On my very first Sunday I met a brown-eyed man who looked me in the eye and said, 'You are a ship captain's daughter. I want you to help me in the sailor's bethel.' This was Madison Edwards...I learned to work with Madison Edwards and his sailors. And the work was wonderful, and Madison Edwards was wonderful in his work. He had learned to remember the faces and names of his sailor friends. He knew their boats and when they were due to go through Vineyard Sound. He met them and if they were not to make port, he threw literature and letters aboard. He particularly liked me because I had been brought up on board ship and could go up the side of the schooners if they did bob up and down.

> We had a large Christian Endeavor Society with a sailor membership. Mr. Edwards gave me the privilege of putting on the pins after the boys had signed the sailor's pledge. One Saturday night a large schooner anchored off Nobska Light. We hoped she would stay there until Sunday afternoon, for we were out of Christian Endeavor pins, but were expecting them on the evening train.

They came, and on Sunday morning right in the middle of the church service, the wind changed. This meant that the schooner anchored off the Light would set sail almost immediately. Mr. Edwards did not wait for the minister to finish his fifteenthly, - he came down the aisle and whispered, 'Miss Jenkins, the wind has changed, and they are making sail out there. Don't you think we could chase them down the Sound since we have those pins, go on board, and hold our meeting and put on the pins?'

We both withdrew, boarded the little steam launch *Helen May* and were off. It was an exciting race, for the *Helen May* was old and sometimes she would go, and then again she wouldn't. But this time she did. We came along side, and thanks to my early training I was soon on board, held our meeting, pinned on the Christian Endeavor tokens and bade the boys God's speed.

Two of those lads never came back. One was badly hurt in shipwreck. He broke his leg and injured his chest. He gave his little Testament to his shipmates and said, 'Take it back to Woods Hole and give it to Madison Edwards, and here's my pin, give it to Miss Jenkins.' I think Mr. Edwards has the little water-soaked Testament in his collection of sailor mementos.[14]

---

14    *Sea Breeze* (34:3) "Address of Mrs. Marsh" April 1922, pp. 44-45.

From the early youth movement of Christian Endeavor, and the creativity and innovation of a few key members in the First Congregational Church in Falmouth, a new concept was born. The idea that grew was that lay-led youth societies did not have to be limited to land, but could become mobile expressions of the Church at sea. Little were they aware of how powerful this idea would grow in the coming years.

*Crew of the Revenue Cutter Fish Hawk, 1908*
Courtesy of B.L. Fisher Library Archives, Asbury Theological Seminary.

---

*Chapter 3*

# Organization and Leadership

---

*There is the sea, vast and spacious,*
*teeming with creatures beyond*
*number—living things both large and*
*small. There the ships go to and fro,*
*and Leviathan, which you formed*
*to frolic there. (Psalm 104:25-26)*

The organization created by Jones and Edwards was simple, but more importantly it relied on lay leadership instead of an organized clergy. Since it built on the work of a youth movement, it also was designed to appeal to the young people of its day, and most sailors on government ships would have been of that same generation of youth. Antoinette Jones described the purpose of the Floating Society, when she wrote,

> While past efforts are not criticized, the aim of Floating Christian Endeavor is to start a man in the Christian life, or, if already a Christian, practically enlist him in Christ's service, with clearly defined duties to God and his shipmates.

> It emphasizes the brotherhood on the
> sea, the fellowship on shore, and makes
> a sailor responsible for a Christian man's
> work wherever he may be, on man-of-
> war, steamship, merchantman, coaster
> or fishing vessel.[15]

The simplicity of the society was based on a
limited number of rules, which could be kept at sea.
The sailor who joined would sign a pledge outlining
these rules. This pledge was adopted from the
regular Christian Endeavor pledge, but Jones and
Edwards added a special phrase about abstaining
from alcohol and profanity. The pledge signed by
members read,

> Trusting in the Lord Jesus Christ for
> strength, I promise Him that I will
> strive to do whatever He would like
> to have me do; that I will pray to Him
> and read the Bible every day; that I
> will try to keep my body clean as the
> "temple of the Holy Ghost" by personal
> purity, total abstinence from alcoholic
> drinks, including wine, beer and cider,
> and profanity, and that, just so far as
> I know how, throughout my whole life,
> I will endeavor to lead a Christian life.
> As a member, I promise to be true to all
> my duties, to be present at and take
> some part, aside from singing, in every
> Christian Endeavor prayer-meeting,
> unless prevented by some reason which
> I can conscientiously give to my Lord
> and Master. If obliged to be absent from

---

15 Antoinette P. Jones, "Floating Societies of Christian
Endeavor," *The Sailors Magazine and Seaman's Friend*,
67:7 (July 1895), 202.

the consecration meeting of the Society,
I will, if possible, send at least a verse of
Scripture to be read in response to my
name at the roll-call.[16]

On joining, the members received a Christian
Endeavor pin by which they made a public statement
and by which they were able to recognize other
members. Members would organize their own
meetings and committees, when possible, and held
each other accountable for their faithfulness to the
pledge. The Floating Christian Endeavor reduced
the number of required committees. There were
essentially two key committees, the lookout
committee, which oversaw membership, joining,
and checking up on absentee members, and the
prayer-meeting committee, which oversaw the
actually meetings that were held on board ship.[17]
In addition, if the society was large enough, they
were encouraged to consider adding a missionary
committee, a temperance committee, a relief
committee, and/or a good literature committee.[18]
In reading a sailor's testimony from the *Thetis*,
Jones quotes,

---

16  *Constitution and By-Laws of the Floating Society of
    Christian Endeavor.* (Boston, MA: The United Society of
    Christian Endeavor, 1890), 13-14.

17  *Ibid.*, 8-10.

18  *Ibid.*, 15-16. In *The Christian Endeavor Manual* by Francis
    Edward Clark, (Boston: United Society of Christian
    Endeavor, 1903), there were three main committees. The
    Floating Christian Endeavor removed the social committee,
    and a host of other suggested committees designed for
    land-based societies, such as the music, flower, Sunday
    school, calling, information, and sunshine committees.

> It is only four months since the Floating Christian Endeavor Committee organized a Floating Christian Endeavor on that ship (the *Thetis*). Since that time the drunken brawls that had been so frequent on board and ashore have become a thing of the past, and in their places are substituted prayer meetings and revivals. I have been twenty-eight years at sea in the darkest scenes of vice with which a sailor is surrounded, and I am convinced that the exhortations of the members of the society are of wonderful influence- sufficient to soften any heart and inclining the hardest sailor to mend his ways.[19]

Jones goes on to indicate that early in the movement requests to form societies would be made to Madison Edwards, who would then pass the requests on to her, and she would arrange the pledges and the society itself.

The first Naval Chaplain to endorse the Floating Christian Endeavor was a Chaplain McLaren who signed the pledge in 1892. After this, various committees were organized in ports to oversee the local work. Local land-based Floating Societies were responsible for the shipboard societies they organized. Their job was primarily to support the ministry to the sailors, to hold meetings on land, and collect funds and items to support the work at sea. These loosely organized local societies would report back to the superintendent, who was Antoinette Jones. Once again, Jones writes,

---

19   Jones, "Floating Societies of Christian Endeavor," 202.

Though Floating Societies on ships report to the committee or worker organizing it, they also report usually to the superintendent of the Floating Christian Endeavor, and thus communication is established between societies, helps are interchanged, and fellowship emphasized. The superintendent is in communication with members and societies in ships in all parts of the world... Where Floating Christian Endeavor Committees are under local Christian Endeavor Unions, the societies composing it pledge assistance in personal work, funds, literature and comfort bags[20]; one Floating Christian Endeavor Committee soliciting and distributing twenty-three hundred in one year.[21]

---

20  Comfort bags were small draw string bags made by ladies on land, which would contain thread, needles, darning wool, scissors, and other useful necessities for sailors, plus a small New Testament with a letter from the maker of the bag and often a religious tract. These items were given out to sailors and were extremely popular among the men at sea. Madison Edwards is once quoted as saying; "I would rather have a thousand comfort bags than the very best evangelist you could send me for the whole season." Bertha Ellen Tuttle, "How to Improve the Condition of the Sailor on Land- Part Second," *Sea Breeze*, 21:2 (January 1909), 37.

21  Jones, "Floating Societies of Christian Endeavor," 203-4.

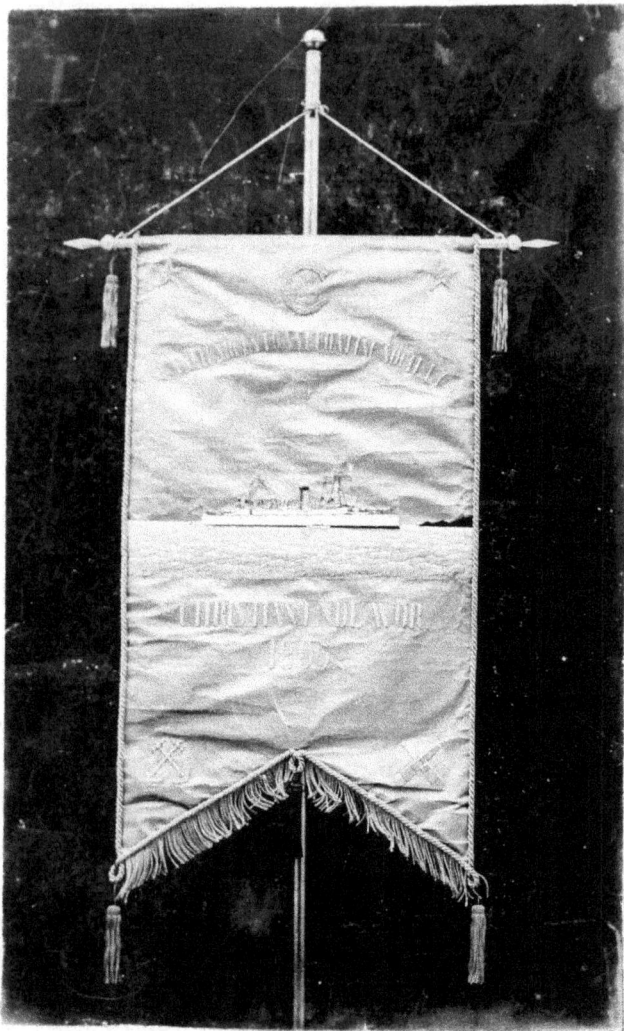

*Banner for the Floating Society
on the* U.S.S. Concord *for the
World Endeavor Convention*
Courtesy of B.L. Fisher Library Archives,
Asbury Theological Seminary.

The dual nature of a Floating Society on land and one on sea is better explained in a news report that described the organization of the Floating Christian Endeavor to its readers this way,

> The organization is two-fold—the regular "floating societies" on land composed largely of Endeavorers interested in this field of missionary work and the societies on individual ships. The latter are always small, and through the constant changes of sea life are generally transient... All naval vessels have chaplains, but the chaplain is an "officer" and the seamen are only men, so there is a gulf there that cannot be bridged to establish genuine fellowship with the chaplain. The Christian Endeavor societies accomplish this, and when officers are members the barriers of rank disappear in the meetings.[22]

This description highlights the importance of a lay-led ministry on board ship, as chaplains frequently ranked higher than common sailors, making fellowship awkward at best.

---

22  Anonymous, "A Pioneer in 'Floating' Work", *San Francisco Call*, 82:43 (13 July, 1897), 3.

*Land-Based Society's Headquarters in Vallejo, CA*
Courtesy of B.L. Fisher Library Archives, Asbury Theological Seminary.

From the very beginning, the Floating Christian Endeavor Society recognized the need to maintain contact with all of their members as much as possible. Being a scattered organization of sailors made this especially difficult, but also crucial, given the lessons from the earlier American Naval Awakening. Jones would send out an annual Christmas and New Year's letter to the members as part of this correspondence. While Antoinette Jones would begin her work with the Floating Christian Endeavor as the Superintendant of the Floating Societies of Christian Endeavor, by 1905 her title was Corresponding Secretary of the Floating Societies of the Christian Endeavor. In 1908, at the formation of the World's Christian Endeavor Union, the World's Floating Christian Endeavor Union was also organized, and Antoinette P. Jones was named president of this organization.[23]

---

23   A.G. Fegert, "Christian Endeavor on Battleships," *Herald of Gospel Liberty*, November 5, 1914, 1439.

The World's Christian Endeavor Union.    Floating Societies of Christian Endeavor.

Merry Christmas.     Happy New Year.

"Charge not thyself with the weight of a year,
  Child of the Master, faithful and dear;
Choose not the cross for the coming week,
  For that is more than He bids thee seek.
Bend not thine arms for tomorrow's load;
  Thou may'st leave that to thy gracious God.
'Daily,' only, He saith to thee,
  'Take up thy cross and follow Me'."

Falmouth, Mass., U. S. A.

*Antoinette D. Jones.*

Corresponding Secretary.

*The 1907 Christmas Greeting from Miss Jones*

Courtesy of B.L. Fisher Library Archives, Asbury Theological Seminary.

Within a very short amount of time, the work of the Floating Societies of the Christian Endeavor blossomed into an elaborate organization, albeit loosely organized in terms of central control. In the notes of her speech before the thirteenth International Christian Endeavor Convention in Cleveland, Ohio, in 1894, Antoinette Jones is recorded as describing the basics of the Floating Societies this way,

> The pledge, our active membership pledge, with inserted clause approved as a declaration of principles, relating to pure living, total abstinence, and non-profanity. Members carry an introduction card, and wear regulation Christian Endeavor badge pin. The constitution is arranged from Model Constitution, and includes covenant for small bands.

> Originally for enlisted men, membership soon extended to sailing vessels.

> Arranged for shipboard, a society ashore in church, mission, or reading-room, composed of sailor members, officered by Christian Endeavor workers, may be called a Floating Society, though as an *organization* it does not 'float.'

> Honor is due established seaman's missions, but missionaries realize how great the harvest, how few the laborers.

> Where new work is advisable, representatives of Christian Endeavor Societies or Local Unions, in ports, form a Floating Christian Endeavor

Committee from consecrated young men and women workers, who receive cordial and practical endorsement from churches and societies.

Subdivisions are necessary when local needs are varied. How work grows as you investigate!

Ship visitation, gospel services on shipboard, dock, and shore: marine hospital services; navy-yard, receiving-ship, training-ship, marine barracks, and naval prison; reading-rooms and boarding-houses. The field may require new reading-room, or launch. Marine missionary services, comfort bag making, collecting good reading and libraries, furnish abundant work for societies ashore.[24]

Reforming the moral character of sailors at sea, was a crucial goal of the Floating Societies. In a witty remark that was picked up and used by others, George Coleman told the 1901 convention of the International Christian Endeavor that the Floating Christian Endeavor was like Ivory Soap, which in the words of the popular advertising phrase of the day was "99 and 44/100 percent pure, and IT FLOATS!"[25]

---

24   Antoinette P. Jones, "Floating Societies of Christian Endeavor," *Official Report of the Thirteenth International Christian Endeavor Convention*, (United Society of Christian Endeavor, Boston, MA. 1894), 47.

25   George W. Coleman, "Christian Endeavor Among Sailors and Soldiers," *Official Report of the Twentieth International Christian Endeavor Convention*, (United Society of Christian Endeavor, Boston, MA. 1901), 114.

Temperance, moral purity, and ending profanity were major religious goals of the organization.

It is also important not to underestimate the importance of the Christian Endeavor pin and its significance. It appears that these were simple regulation Christian Endeavor pins, and not items designed especially for the Floating Societies. Since they appear in a number of photos, they were apparently permitted on naval uniforms and were also worn with a certain degree of pride. Antoinette Jones is quoted in an article as saying that a sailor told her, "five years ago it was a rare thing to find a Christian man in the naval service, but that now it was not a rare thing to see a Christian Endeavor pin on a sailor's uniform."[26]

In his speech at the 21st International Christian Endeavor Convention, ex-Navy Chaplain Robert E. Steele, reported,

> Floating Christian Endeavor stands for faithful testimony on board ship. Its members are marked men. The little badge worn on the blue uniform speaks constantly to all on board, telling that one at least is not ashamed to own his Master and his Lord.
>
> Floating Christian Endeavor knows no church save the church invisible. Differing from the Society on land, it is the fruit that grows directly from the vine, rather than from the branches. Its point of union is loyalty to Christ. Church organization is impossible afloat.

26 Anonymous, "A Pioneer in 'Floating' Work," 3.

> Many most sincere Christian sailors are
> not members of any church.
>
> It is a sufficient test of sincerity for
> a man on shipboard to be willing to
> take the pledge, and wear the pin of
> the Society. The hypocrite is a fungus
> which does not long endure the fire of
> persecution at sea. A Christian sailor is
> under constant observation. A thousand
> eyes mark every word, every action.
> There is nothing to be gained by a false
> profession of faith in Christ, therefore
> Christian sailors are usually true stuff.
> Unite these men, identify them, and
> you have organized a mighty agency for
> evangelization.[27]

Steele goes on to point out that Floating
Christian Endeavor is not about mission *to* sailors,
which had been tried in the past, but the mission
*of* sailors to other men of the sea, which once again
highlights the lay-led nature of this "church" upon
the sea. The entire concept was not to do mission
work for sailors, but rather to empower laymen
who were sailors to evangelize other sailors at sea,
and thus enlarge the Church in the process of their
daily lives. Francis Clark also points out that at the
time, this was the only major religious work among
sailors in the navy. He writes,

---

27 Anonymous, "Floating Endeavor as an Evangelistic
Agency," *The Story of the Denver Convention: Being the
Official Report of the Twenty-First International Christian
Endeavor Convention held in Tent Endeavor and Many
Churches, Denver, Colo. July 9-13, 1903,* (United Society
of Christian Endeavor, Boston, MA. 1903), 65-66.

The Young Men's Christian Associations are doing most admirable service, but on the sea are largely social in their functions. Christian Endeavor in the navy insists upon outspoken religion, and the badge which sailors are proud to wear, though they are often ridiculed by their companions for wearing it, stands for 'Christ Exalted' there as everywhere else.[28]

28  Francis Clark, *Christian Endeavor in all Lands: A Record of Twenty-Five Years of Progress*, (W.E. Scull, 1906), 468.

S.M. Smith, U.S.A.S.
Solace, *wearing a Christian
Endeavor pin at his neck*
Courtesy of B.L. Fisher Library Archives,
Asbury Theological Seminary.

*Chapter 4*

# The Spanish-
# American War

*In my distress I called to the Lord, and
he answered me. From deep in the
realm of the dead I called for help,
and you listened to my cry. You hurled
me into the depths, into the very
heart of the seas, and the currents
swirled about me; all your waves and
breakers swept over me. (Jonah 2:2-3)*

In 1898, the United States went to war with
the declining Spanish Empire. This ten-week war
started with rebellions in Cuba against Spanish
control that were supported by the United States.
Popular sentiment was inflamed by newspaper
journalism and a mysterious explosion on the *U.S.S.
Maine* in Havana Harbor, which led to the death
of 266 sailors and the sinking of the ship. Spain
rejected President William McKinley's demands for
Spain to leave Cuba and war resulted.

When the war ended with the Treaty of Paris,
the U.S. was left occupying Spain's former colonies
of Cuba, Puerto Rico, Guam, and the Philippines.

Commodore Dewey on the *U.S.S. Olympia* destroyed the Spanish squadron in Manila Bay, while Captain Henry Glass on the *U.S.S. Charleston* took Guam in the Pacific. Rear Admiral Sampson on the *U.S.S. New York* helped the invasion of Puerto Rico with a blockade of San Juan Bay and then proceeded to Cuba to destroy the Spanish Caribbean Squadron at the Battle of Santiago de Cuba.

From this war, Teddy Roosevelt would emerge as a rising national hero and political star, while the United States became a colonial power in the dying days of colonialism. The United States also emerged as a naval power to be dealt with in the 20th century.

During this war several cases of sailors in the Floating Christian Endeavor became publicized in the U.S. Most notably was Carlton H. Jencks, a sailor who had originally been on the *U.S.S. Charleston* and helped found the Christian Endeavor Seaman's Home at Nagasaki, Japan. He was eighteen years old when the *Charleston* was detained in Nagasaki for ten months. Realizing there was no place for young Christian sailors to stay in the port,[29] Jencks and fellow Floating Christian Endeavor members, working with local missionaries, raised the money

---

29  *Ibid.*, 464. Francis Clark writes,
   The boys of the society soon found, when on shore leave, that there was no place in all the great city of Nagasaki where a decent sailor could get a meal or a night's lodging. There were respectable first-class hotels, but these were beyond their means. All the other places were low dives and dram-shops, and one street where these are especially numerous in Nagasaki is known to this day as 'Bloody street'.

to buy and furnish the home.[30] After his time on the *Charleston*, Jencks was transferred to the *U.S.S. Maine* as a gunner's mate. Carlton H. Jencks was one of the many lost when the *Maine* was sunk in Havana, Cuba on February 15, 1898 leading to the start of the Spanish-American War and its rallying cry, "Remember the *Maine!*" He was twenty-one years old when he died.[31]

---

30  A.G. Fegert, "Christian Endeavor on Battleships," 1439.

31  George W. Coleman, "Christian Endeavor Among Sailors and Soldiers," 114. Two other Floating Christian Endeavor members died on the *Maine*. A brief article in the *New York Times* from February 22, 1898 notes that,

One of (Jencks) associates on the *Maine* was Elmer Meilstrup, eighteen years of age, who became a member of the floating society, Dec. 19, 1897. He intended to prepare for the ministry after leaving the Navy. Another was William Rushforth, who was the delegate for the *Thetis* floating society and represented the San Diego Endeavor work at the Boston convention in 1895.

*The Endeavor group on the U.S.S. Charleston* Jencks is holding the parasol. Courtesy of B. L. Fisher Library Archives, Asbury Theological Seminary.

In another publicized case, there were twelve members of the Floating Christian Endeavor on the *U.S.S. Olympia* with Admiral Dewey when he fought the battle of Manila Bay.[32] The battle was fought on May 1, 1898, when Dewey destroyed the Spanish Pacific fleet and took the Philippines as a U.S. colony. In an article in *The New York Times*, it was reported,

> Miss A.P. Jones of Falmouth, Mass., has long kept up Endeavor work by correspondence among sailors. There is a Floating Society of the Nagasaki (Japan) Christian Endeavor Home for Seamen. From this society there went out fifteen men among the marines of the *Olympia*. At Cavite these fifteen men have increased in numbers to almost 100, and since the victory at Manila they have been active in religious work among their fellows.[33]

After speaking about the Floating Christian Endeavor Societies at the Denver convention in 1903, ex-chaplain Robert E. Steele of the U.S. Navy presented Francis Clark with the first American flag flown over the Philippines from the Christian Endeavorers in the Navy. The account reads,

> After the battle of Manila, when the Spanish force had surrendered, Admiral Dewey sent a squad of marines under a lieutenant to hoist an American flag over

---

32 George W. Coleman, "Christian Endeavor Among Sailors and Soldiers," 115.
33 "Religious News and Views," *The New York Times*, June 11, 1898.

Cavite, the first fortress to fall. Two of
these men were Christian Endeavorers.
One of them climbed the battlements
of the fort and raised the flag. When it
was lowered to be replaced by a larger
flag, it came into possession of himself
and his comrade. He was killed in a
skirmish battle a few months later and
the comrade gave the flag to Chaplain
Steele to be presented to the Christian
Endeavorers, as a sign of their need for
the work of the Society in the Navy.[34]

---

34   Anonymous, "Floating Endeavor as an Evangelistic Agency,"
     66-67.
     It is also interesting to note the following account,
         The morning of 3 May brought information from shore
     that the Spanish land forces and the naval personnel ashore
     at Cavite from the sunken ships had evacuated the Cavite
     arsenal and the town of Cavite. Comm. Dewey ordered
     the captain of the *Baltimore* to land an MD to take charge
     of the arsenal and town of Cavite and to protect property
     there.
         That morning a detachment of *Baltimore* Marines,
     commanded by 1st Lt. Dion Williams, landed at Cavite,
     establishing a guard over the station and especially the
     arsenal.
         As soon as order was restored in the arsenal and town
     the Stars and Stripes were hoisted on the flagstaff at the
     arsenal while the Marine guard presented arms and the
     bugler sounded "To the Colors." This was the first flag
     hoisted on Spanish soil in the Spanish-American War and
     the halliards were manned by Sgt. James Grant and Cpl.
     Joseph Poe. The flag was preserved and afterward turned
     over to Dewey, who sent it to the Naval Academy with a
     letter stating the facts concerning it.
     George B. Clark, *Battle History of the United States Marine
     Corps, 1775-1945*, (Jefferson, NC: McFarland 2010), 87-88.
     The two stories do not necessarily have to be contradictory.
     There was a Floating Christian Endeavor Society on the
     *Baltimore*, as well as on the *Olympia* and the *Raleigh*,
     which also fought in the Battle of Manila. The larger

*American Flag*
Flag presented to Clark by Chaplain
Steele at the Denver Convention in 1903.
Photo courtesy of B.L. Fisher Library
Archives, Asbury Theological Seminary.

Albert Marquardt, another of the members of
the Floating Christian Endeavor on the *Olympia*,

---

official flag may be the flag sent by Dewey to the Naval
Academy, while the smaller flag given to Steele may have
been a more informal flag flown by the marines before the
official flag was raised. A smaller naval flag, documented
as that given to Clark in 1903, is part of the Christian
Endeavor Collection in the B.L. Fisher Library Archives.

went on to become a missionary to miners in Colorado.[35]

There were also Floating Christian Endeavor members aboard the *U.S.S. Oregon*, when in 1898 she had to make a rapid journey from the Pacific Ocean to Cuba around the tip of South America.[36] She did the journey of 13,675 nautical miles in 66 days, which was amazing for the day, and the feat was recognized nationally. The vessel then fought at the Battle of Santiago de Cuba and earned the nickname, "The Bulldog of the Navy." The dramatic need to move the *Oregon* from the Pacific Ocean to the Caribbean was one of the motivating factors behind the decision to build the Panama Canal.

---

35  A.G. Fegert, "Christian Endeavor on Battleships," 1439.
36  George W. Coleman, "Christian Endeavor Among Sailors and Soldiers," 115.

*William Elitson of the*
U.S.S. Olympia
Notice this sailor is wearing a Christian
Endeavor pin directly above the
"Dewey Medal" awarded to sailors
who fought in the Battle of Manila
Bay. The *Olympia* was Dewey's flagship.
Courtesy of B.L. Fisher Library Archives,
Asbury Theological Seminary.

*Michael Kehke of the*
**U.S.S. Oregon,** *1896*
Notice in this image, the Christian Endeavor
pin worn on the knot of his necktie.
Courtesy of B.L. Fisher Library Archives,
Asbury Theological Seminary.

Following the Spanish-American War, President Theodore Roosevelt modernized the Navy, and to demonstrate the U.S. military power on the seas following the defeat of Spain, a fleet of modern battleships was sent to travel around the world. The sixteen battleships with additional support vessels left on December 16, 1907 and returned on February 22, 1909. Called the "Great White Fleet" because of the white paint used on the vessels, this exhibition of military power also contained Floating Christian Endeavor Societies on at least two vessels, the *Vermont* and the *Nebraska*. A fireman from the *Vermont* Society, E. Ray Sanders, was made the president of the "Fleet Union of Floating Endeavorers" for all of the ships in the "Great White Fleet". He was even granted a special pass by the admiral to visit the other ships as desired.[37] On returning, Sanders along with Antoinette Jones spoke in New York City along with a British Floating Christian Endeavor member from the British ship, *Inflexible*.[38]

---

37   John F. Cowan, "Christian Endeavor," *The Friend* (Board of the Hawaiian Evangelical Association), 65:10 (October 1908), 10.

38   Anonymous, "Sailors in the Pulpit," *New York Times*, Monday, October 4, 1909, 20.

*Group of the Floating Christian
Endeavor on board the* Vermont
*When it was sailing as part
of the Great White Fleet*
E. Ray Sanders, who was chosen to
lead all of the Endeavor sailors on the
fleet, is in the back row on the far
left. Courtesy of B.L. Fisher Library
Archives, Asbury Theological Seminary.

*Chapter 5*

# Growth and Decline of the Floating Christian Endeavor

*The seas have lifted up, Lord, the
seas have lifted up their voice; the
seas have lifted up their pounding
waves. Mightier than the thunder
of the great waters, mightier than
the breakers of the sea—the Lord
on high is mighty. (Psalm 93: 3-4)*

On the success of the Floating Christian Endeavor, Francis Clark, the founder of Christian Endeavor, wrote,

> That a society which seems so peculiarly wedded to a local church, with its pledge of constancy and its forms of service, many of which, from their very nature, can be performed only upon dry land, should find its place on ships of war and merchant vessels, and thus go into every harbor of the world is indeed surprising. It is only another illustration of God's

guiding hand, and of the flexibility of
the Society and its adaptability to all
classes and conditions of men.[39]

In a short span of eleven years, the work
had grown tremendously, not due to the work of
traditional missionaries or an ordained chaplaincy.
It grew because of to the flexibility of a lay-led
movement accompanied by the transient nature of
the mission field and a genuine passion for Christ
in its members. The movement quickly spread
internationally as well, with Clark mentioning
Floating Christian Endeavor Societies on British
and Japanese vessels. Antoinette Jones mentions
societies on ships from Canada, New Zealand,
Australia, and one society, "among the marines of
the Imperial Japanese Navy, whose members in the
recent war, went to the front, two of whom were
killed."[40] In a report on the work of the Christian
Endeavor among sailors and soldiers, one writer
notes,

> But if Christian Endeavor made rapid
> progress on land, what shall we say of
> its floating capacity on the seas. Think
> of the sailor's reputation for wild living,
> remember the loneliness of his calling,
> his freedom from restraint when going
> ashore, and then let me tell you that
> over 150 floating societies of Christian
> Endeavor have been organized and
> more than 6000 sailor lads have taken

---

39  Francis Clark, *Christian Endeavor in all Lands,* 462-3.
40  Antoinette P. Jones, "Address of Miss Antoinette P. Jones,"
    *Official Report of the Fourteenth International Christian
    Endeavor Convention,* (United Society of Christian
    Endeavor, Boston, MA. 1895), 65.

their Christian Endeavor pledge. Now remember, too, a sailor's opportunity for meeting many peoples, and imagine, if you can, what a force for righteousness 6000 sailor-men can exert in the world.[41]

However, the very factors that made the Floating Christian Endeavor such a success were also a major weakness. First, the overall nature of the Floating Christian Endeavor Societies was temporary. As Francis Clark wrote, "Some of them (Floating Christian Endeavor Societies) necessarily have but a short life, for the sailors are changed from ship to ship; their terms expire, or for other unavoidable reasons the societies are often broken. Floating Societies must be frequently reorganized."[42]

41  George W. Coleman, "Christian Endeavor Among Sailors and Soldiers," 114.
42  Francis Clark, *Christian Endeavor in all Lands,* 463.

| Year | Number of Members | Number of Societies |
|------|-------------------|---------------------|
| 1901 | 6000 | 150 |
| 1900 | no numbers reported | no numbers reported[*] |
| 1899 | no numbers reported | 123 |
| 1898 | no numbers reported | 119 |
| 1897 | no numbers reported | 91 |
| 1896 | no numbers reported | 80[**] |
| 1895 | 3000 | 71 |
| 1894 | 2000 | 51 |
| 1893 | no numbers reported | 21 |
| 1892 | 200 | no numbers reported |
| 1891 | no numbers reported | 4 |
| 1890 | no numbers reported | no numbers reported |

*Early Growth of The Floating
Christian Endeavor*
Based on numbers reported at Annual
International Conventions of the Christian
Endeavor Society, either in the text of
speeches or in the tables of statistics.[43]

43  *So far, I have been unable to locate a report on the
International Convention held in 1900 in London, and
therefore I am unable to note any numbers from this
report, but they most likely do exist in print somewhere.
**This is the only case where conflicting information
appears in the text of convention speeches and in the
table of statistics. In the speech for this year's convention,
the number of societies is given at 47 and not 80, as
reported in the statistics. Given the general growth trend,
80 seems the more reliable number.

Secondly, the flexibility of the organization that allowed it to adapt to life on the sea, was only loosely organized and connected to the oversight of one woman, Antoinette Jones, first as superintendant, later as corresponding secretary, and then president of the World's Floating Christian Endeavor Union. Without her at the helm, there was just a coalition of smaller local societies each doing their own work locally. She does not appear to have had much of a staff or organization to support her work, even though she was held in high regard. In one place, recording an illustrated lecture being given, the writer notes, "The audience was particularly pleased with a fine picture showing, in her own home, which has been an altar of devotion to the welfare of the boys in our navy and merchant marine, Miss Antoinette Jones, Falmouth, Mass., the 'sister' of every sailor afloat."[44]

Thirdly, the lack of an ordained leadership on board ship left the sustaining work of building a congregation and maintaining it during periods of weakness and stress solely in the hands of untrained and often untested Christian laymen. In some cases where inspired leadership rose up from the ranks, as with Carlton Jencks and his work in Nagasaki, the Floating Christian Endeavor Society worked brilliantly, but one must wonder as well how many smaller organized societies fell apart without adequate leadership and guidance.

---

44 Anonymous, "Floating Endeavor and the Stereopticon," *The Story of the Denver Convention: Being the Official Report of the Twenty-First International Christian Endeavor Convention held in Tent Endeavor and Many Churches, Denver, Colo. July 9-13, 1903*, (United Society of Christian Endeavor, Boston, MA. 1903), 137.

Floating Endeavor Society on the U.S.S. Chicago
Image in the Public Domain.

While Antoinette Jones was the visible leader and organizer of the Floating Christian Endeavor, co-founder Madison Edwards remained committed to the work of the Floating Societies of the Christian Endeavor. As noted by Francis Clark,

> The Endeavor launches at San Diego, at Vineyard Haven, where Captain Edwards has been such a Christian Endeavor power for good among the sailors, and at many other places have been real steam messengers of the gospel, which they have carried to a multitude of hardy men who sail the seas.[45]

Edwards even attended the Fourteenth International Christian Endeavor Convention, held in Boston in 1895, where the report states, "Mr. Madison Edwards, Vineyard Haven, who has experienced helpfulness in the use of the pledge, gave form of receiving new members and donning pin, with Scripture motto."[46]

---

45  Francis Clark, *Christian Endeavor in all Lands*, 471.
46  Anonymous, "Conference of Floating Societies of Christian Endeavor," *Official Report of the Fourteenth International Christian Endeavor Convention*, (United Society of Christian Endeavor, Boston, MA. 1895), 213.

*An Older Madison Edwards*
*Wearing a Hold Fast Pin*
From the Author's Collection

Edwards did however move his ministry from Woods Hole to Vineyard Haven on Martha's Vineyard, where he worked out of the Seaman's Bethel and Reading Room. He continued to be interested in the work of the Floating Christian Endeavor on the larger ships, but his work in Vineyard Haven was mostly with sailors on ships with smaller, more transient crews, where Christian fellowships, like the Floating Christian Endeavor would not work as well. Edwards remained convinced of the need for Christian fellowship on the water and not just in the ports, and so he established the Hold Fast Society in 1907, based on many of the same concepts of the Floating Christian Endeavor, to meet that need.[47]

Some of the local work was able to transition with changing times within their local context. For example, in 1902 a Captain Charles Farr started a work for sailors in San Pedro, California, which became a part of the Floating Christian Endeavor. This work was ultimately taken over by John Makins.[48] About 1945 it transitioned to becoming a regular rescue mission, and as "Beacon Light Mission" it continues to this day, even though it relocated out of San Pedro for Wilmington, California in 1970.[49]

---

47  George Wiseman, They *Kept the Lower Lights Burning: The Story of the Seaman's Bethel and its Chaplains*, 99-100.

48  John Makins had been the superintendent of the Christian Endeavor Seaman's Home in Nagasaki, Japan and spoke at the Twenty-First International Convention in Denver, CO.

49  See the Beacon Light Mission history webpage for more information,    http://www.beaconlightmission.org/blm_history.html.

*Endeavor Lunch Counter, San Pedro, CA*
Courtesy of B.L. Fisher Library Archives, Asbury Theological Seminary.

In general however, the Floating Christian Endeavor Societies seemed to fade into obscurity around the time of World War I. This could be accounted for in a number of ways. First, the transitory nature of this lay-lead ministry made it fragile to begin with, but with the onset of World War I, it may have been impossible to organize on board naval ships and maintain the societies due to massive movements of troops and wartime conditions. Second, the growth in organized ministries to sailors through the growth of official chaplains for the U.S. Navy and the work of more tightly organized groups like the Y.M.C.A. may have supplanted the need for the Floating Christian Endeavor. Third, Miss Antoinette P. Jones was a guiding force, co-founder, speaker, and corresponding secretary for the Floating Christian Endeavor, and she died December 15, 1918 at age 62 during the influenza epidemic just at the end of the war. In a report to the Boston Seaman's Friend Society, Madison Edwards reported,

> On December 19, the funeral of Miss Antoinette P. Jones, world's superintendent of the Floating Christian Endeavor, was conducted in Falmouth, her home town. Rev. Mr. Baker, pastor of the Congregational Church of that town, who had charge of the funeral, called upon the Chaplain of the Vineyard Sound Mission to offer remarks, stating that he was the person who started her upon her lifework for seamen. In 1890 she became interested in the sailor-work that was being carried on at Woods Hole, and with her help the Floating Christian Endeavor was organized. It started with

little societies on the revenue cutters *Dexter* and *Gallatin*. From that very small beginning it has gone out into all parts of the world. The large ships of war in the English, German, and United States navies have their little bands of Floating Christian Endeavorers. Miss Jones corresponded with all of these, and had vital interest in every one of them. The work in Japan was as familiar to her as the work in the homeland. She was most devoted to her work, and that without compensation. Many a sailor boy has been helped to a higher education through her instrumentality.[50]

Her death, combined with the other factors at the end of World War I may have prevented a successful reorganization of the group following the war. In addition, many of the smaller local organizations had branched out with similar ministries, such as Edward's Hold Fast Society and the Boston Seaman's Friend Society's Anchor Alliance, which were now independent of any larger umbrella institution.

While the overall period of time in which the Floating Christian Endeavor was active was relatively short, it did provide a crucial link in the chain of missions to men at sea. It sought to empower sailors, as with the earlier American Naval Awakening, to take charge of their own spiritual lives on board government vessels, but it also provided a better organization through

---

50  Madison Edwards, "Madison Edwards, Vineyard Haven," *The Sea Breeze* (Boston Seaman's Friend Society), 31:2 (January 1919), 24-25.

Miss Jones' land-based societies and through a network of land-based chaplains, such as Madison Edwards. This organization was flexible enough to allow societies to form in difficult situations, but provided enough structure to help maintain a lay-led "church" on board each vessel. This flexibility is seen in the development of organizations like Edwards' Hold Fast Society, and the Beacon Light Mission in California, which spun off from local Floating Christian Endeavor societies.

The growth of the organized naval chaplaincy and relief organizations that developed or grew during World War I, such as the Red Cross and the YMCA made many aspects of the Floating Christian Endeavor unnecessary. However, the growth of globalism and transnationalism on land, as well as on sea, still demands flexible models of the church that can be led and organized by lay people on the move. Despite the challenges of time, the Floating Christian Endeavor Society still offers a viable model worth considering for current models of mission in complex social environments.

# Works Cited

Anonymous

    1890    *Constitution and By-Laws of the Floating Society of Christian Endeavor*, Boston, MA: The United Society of Christian Endeavor.

    1895    "Conference of Floating Societies of Christian Endeavor," *Official Report of the Fourteenth International Christian Endeavor Convention*. Boston, MA: The United Society of Christian Endeavor.

    1897    "A Pioneer in 'Floating' Work," *San Francisco Call*, 82:43 (13 July, 1897): 3.

    1898    "Religious News and Views," *The New York Times*, June 11, 1898.

    1903    "Floating Endeavor and the Stereopticon," *The Story of the Denver Convention: Being the Official Report of the Twenty-First International Christian Endeavor Convention held in Tent Endeavor and Many Churches, Denver, Colo. July 9-13, 1903*, Boston, MA: The United Society of Christian Endeavor: 137.

    1909    "Sailors in the Pulpit," *New York Times*, Monday, October 4, 1909: 20.

1922     "Address of Mrs. Marsh," *Sea Breeze* (Boston Seaman's Friend Society), 34(3): 44-45 (April).

Clark, Francis E.
1895     *World Wide Endeavor: The Story of the Young People's Society of Christian Endeavor from the Beginning and in all Lands.* Philadelphia, PA: Gillespie & Metzgar.

1903     *The Christian Endeavor Manual.* Boston, MA: The United Society of Christian Endeavor.

1906     *Christian Endeavor in all Lands: A Record of Twenty-Five Years of Progress.* W.E. Scull.

Clark, George B.
2010     *Battle History of the United States Marine Corps, 1775-1945.* Jefferson, NC: McFarland.

Coleman, George W.
1901     "Christian Endeavor Among Sailors and Soldiers," *Official Report of the Twentieth International Christian Endeavor Convention,* Boston, MA: The United Society of Christian Endeavor: 114.

Cowan, John F.
1908     "Christian Endeavor," *The Friend* (Board of the Hawaiian Evangelical Association), 65 (10): 10 (October).

Crawford, Mary Caroline
1906     "The World for Christ," *National Magazine,* February: 473-483.

Drury, Clifford Merrill
1948     *The History of the Chaplain Corps, United States Navy, Vol. 3. United States Navy Chaplains.* Washington DC: U.S. Government Printing Office.

Edwards, Madison
  1919    "Madison Edwards, Vineyard Haven," *The Sea Breeze* (Boston Seaman's Friend Society), 31(2):24-25 (January).

Fegert, A.G.
  1914    "Christian Endeavor on Battleships," *Herald of Gospel Liberty*, November 5, 1914: 1439.

Jones, Antoinette P.
  1894    "Floating Societies of Christian Endeavor," *Official Report of the Thirteenth International Christian Endeavor Convention*, Boston, MA: The United Society of Christian Endeavor: 47.

  1895a   "Address of Miss Antoinette P. Jones," *Official Report of the Fourteenth International Christian Endeavor Convention*, Boston, MA: The United Society of Christian Endeavor: 65.

  1895b   "Floating Societies of Christian Endeavor," *The Sailors Magazine and Seaman's Friend*, 67(7): 202 (July).

Kverndal, Roald
  1986    *Seamen's Missions: Their Origin and Early Growth.* Pasedena, CA: William Carey Library.

  2008    *The Way of the Sea: The Changing Shape of Mission in the Seafaring World.* Pasedena, CA: William Carey Library.

Showalter, Douglas K.
  2001    "Antoinette Palmer Jones: The Goodness and Power of One Christian," *Spiritsail* 25(2): 23-31.

Tuttle, Bertha Ellen
1909    "How to Improve the Condition of the Sailor on Land- Part Second," *Sea Breeze* (Boston Seaman's Friend Society), 21(2):37 (January).

Wiseman, George
ca 1976 *They Kept the Lower Lights Burning: The Story of the Seaman's Bethel and its Chaplains.* <http://place.asburyseminary.edu/academicbooks/1/>

# Images Cited

"Dr. Francis E. Clark, Founder of Christian Endeavor" on page 9. Crawford: The World for Christ. Image in the public domain.

"Early Image of Madison Edwards" on page 12. Image from the Author's Collection.

"Pen Sketch of Miss Antoinette Jones" on page 13. Image in the Public Domain.

"The Helen May in its Days in Woods Hole" on page 14. Courtesy of B.L. Fisher Library Archives, Asbury Theological Seminary. <http://place. asburyseminary.edu/fscephotos/3/>

A clearer copy of this image is found in Francis Clark's *World Wide Endeavor: The Story of the Young People's Society of Christian Endeavor from the Beginning and in all Lands* (Philadelphia, PA: Gillespie & Metzgar, 1895), 361. It clearly shows that the young lady at the stern of the boat is holding a flag with the characteristic entwined C and E of the Christian Endeavor logo.

"Crew of the Revenue Cutter Fish Hawk, 1908" on page 18. Courtesy of B.L. Fisher Library Archives, Asbury Theological Seminary. < http://place. asburyseminary.edu/fscephotos/20/>

Not all of the Floating Christian Endeavor Societies were on large naval ships. One society was aboard the *U.S.S. Fish Hawk*, a small government vessel built specifically to do government work for the Fisheries Commission. It was designed as a floating hatchery and laboratory, one of the first of its kind.

"Banner for the Floating Society on the U.S.S. Concord for the World Endeavor Convention" on page 24. Courtesy of B.L. Fisher Library Archives, Asbury Theological Seminary. < http://place. asburyseminary.edu/fscephotos/15/>

"Land-Based Society's Headquarters in Vallejo, CA" on page 26. Courtesy of B.L. Fisher Library Archives, Asbury Theological Seminary. < http:// place.asburyseminary.edu/fscephotos/23/>

"The 1907 Christmas Greeting from Miss Jones" on page 28. Courtesy of B.L. Fisher Library Archives, Asbury Theological Seminary. < http://place. asburyseminary.edu/fscephotos/5/>

"S.M. Smith, U.S.A.S. Solace, wearing a Christian Endeavor pin at his neck" on page 34. Courtesy of B.L. Fisher Library Archives, Asbury Theological Seminary. <http://place.asburyseminary.edu/ fscephotos/10/>

"The Endeavor group on the U.S.S. Charleston" on page 38. Courtesy of B.L. Fisher Library Archives, Asbury Theological Seminary. < http://place. asburyseminary.edu/fscephotos/6/>

In this photo, taken in Nagasaki, Japan, Carlton Jencks is pictured with other Floating Christian Endeavor crewmen from the *Charleston* in Japanese clothing.

"American Flag" on page 41"William Elitson of the U.S.S. Olympia" on page 43. Courtesy of B.L. Fisher Library Archives, Asbury Theological Seminary. < http://place.asburyseminary.edu/christianedeavor/3/>

"William Elitson of the U.S.S. Olympia" on page 43. Courtesy of B.L. Fisher Library Archives, Asbury Theological Seminary. < http://place.asburyseminary.edu/fscephotos/8/>

"Michael Kehke of the U.S.S. Oregon, 1896" on page 44. Courtesy of B.L. Fisher Library Archives, Asbury Theological Seminary. < http://place.asburyseminary.edu/fscephotos/9/>

"Group of the Floating Christian Endeavor on board the Vermont When it was sailing as part of the Great White Fleet" on page 46. Courtesy of B.L. Fisher Library Archives, Asbury Theological Seminary. < http://place.asburyseminary.edu/fscephotos/37/>

"Floating Endeavor Society on the U.S.S. Chicago" on page 52. Crawford: The World for Christ. Image in the public domain. From Crawford, "The World for Christ," pp. 479.

"An Older Madison Edwards Wearing a Hold Fast Pin" on page 54. From the Author's Collection.

"Endeavor Lunch Counter, San Pedro, CA" on page 56. Courtesy of B.L. Fisher Library Archives, Asbury Theological Seminary. < http://place.asburyseminary.edu/fscephotos/14/>

www.ingramcontent.com/pod-product-compliance
Lightning Source LLC
Chambersburg PA
CBHW060651030426
42337CB00017B/2557